U.S. GOVERNMENT AGENCIES

WHAT DOES THE FBI DO?

DANIELLE HAYNES

Published in 2026 by The Rosen Publishing Group, Inc.
2544 Clinton Street, Buffalo, NY 14224

Copyright © 2026 by The Rosen Publishing Group, Inc.

All rights reserved. No part of this book may be reproduced in any form without permission in writing from the publisher, except by a reviewer.

First Edition

Editor: Danielle Haynes
Book Design: Rachel Rising

Photo Credits: Cover, Nes/iStock.com; Cover, pp. 8, 11, 13, 15, 20 chrisdorney/Shutterstock.com; Cover, pp. 1, 3–24 Madan Designer/Shutterstock.com; Cover, pp. 1, 3–24 Art Posting/Shutterstock.com; p. 4 dizain/Shutterstock.com; p. 5 blvdone/Shutterstock.com; p. 6 Gorodenkoff/Shutterstock.com; pp. 7, 13 Pressmaster/Shutterstock.com; p. 9 https://commons.wikimedia.org/wiki/File:Charles_Joseph_Bonaparte,_1851-1921_LCCN2001704024.jpg; p. 9 https://commons.wikimedia.org/wiki/File:Stanley_Wellington_Finch,_head-and-shoulders_portrait,_facing_slightly_left.jpg; p. 10 danielfela/Shutterstock.com; p. 11 DT phots1/Shutterstock.com; p. 11 https://commons.wikimedia.org/wiki/File:Kash_Patel,_official_FBI_portrait_(cropped_1).jpg; p. 12 Leonard Zhukovsky/Shutterstock.com; p. 15 Stephen Reeves/Shutterstock.com; p. 16 Maryna Marchenko/Shutterstock.com; p. 17 digicomfoto/Shutterstock.com; p. 18 Indypendenz/Shutterstock.com; p. 19 Gigi Delgado/Shutterstock.com; p. 20 Fer Gregory/Shutterstock.com; p. 21 https://commons.wikimedia.org/wiki/File:FBI_Academy.jpg.

Cataloging-in-Publication Data

Names: Haynes, Danielle.
Title: What does the FBI do? / Danielle Haynes.
Description: Buffalo, New York : PowerKids Press, 2026. | Series: U.S. government agencies | Includes glossary and index.
Identifiers: ISBN 9781499453089 (pbk.) | ISBN 9781499453096 (library bound) | ISBN 9781499453102 (ebook)
Subjects: LCSH: United States. Federal Bureau of Investigation–Juvenile literature. | Criminal investigation–United States–Juvenile literature.
Classification: LCC HV8144.F43 H38 2026 | DDC 363.250973–dc23

Manufactured in the United States of America

Some of the images in this book illustrate individuals who are models. The depictions do not imply actual situations or events.

CPSIA Compliance Information: Batch #CSPK26. For Further Information contact Rosen Publishing at 1-800-237-9932.

CONTENTS

WHAT IS THE FBI?. 4

FEDERAL LAW
ENFORCEMENT. 6

BIRTH OF THE FBI 8

DEPARTMENT OF JUSTICE 10

FBI BY THE NUMBERS 12

BAPTIST STREET
CHURCH BOMBING. 14

TECHNOLOGY 16

A CAREER WITH THE FBI. 18

GLOSSARY 22

FOR MORE INFORMATION 23

INDEX 24

WHAT IS THE FBI?

Police officers play an important role in society. They work to keep people safe and stop crimes. Police officers are usually pretty easy to identify by their uniforms. But did you know there are many different kinds of police, or law enforcement officers?

Your local police are probably the most common officers you see. They work for the city or town. There are also law enforcement officers at the **county** level. These officers work for the sheriff's office. There are also state police.

Finally, there are federal law enforcement officers, many whom work for the Federal Bureau of Investigation, or FBI.

The FBI headquarters is in Washington, D.C., and is named after one of the agency's first directors, J. Edgar Hoover.

FEDERAL LAW ENFORCEMENT

Federal law enforcement in the United States is nearly as old as the country itself. The first federal police agency was the U.S. Marshals Service. The U.S. Congress formed the Marshals Service with the **Judiciary** Act of 1789. This agency still exists today and is mostly responsible for finding criminals and transporting prisoners.

The country needs federal police to help enforce federal laws, which are sometimes different than state and local laws. Sometimes, different levels of law enforcement work together on the same case. Kidnapping, for example, is usually a state crime. But if the kidnapper takes a person from one state to another, it then becomes a federal crime.

Different kinds of police have different jurisdictions, or areas of responsibility. The FBI's jurisdiction is the whole country, while your local police is responsible just for your city.

BIRTH OF THE FBI

By the early 20th century, the U.S. government realized it needed a more robust federal law enforcement agency. The country had spread coast to coast and cities were rapidly growing. Crime was also growing.

The FBI observes its founding as July 26, 1908. This was when U.S. Attorney General Charles Bonaparte hired a force of agents to handle investigations for the Department of Justice (DOJ). The agency underwent many changes—including names—but by 1935, it became the FBI. The first person to lead the FBI was Stanley Finch. At the time, this position was called chief examiner. Today the FBI leader is called director.

AGENCY INSIGHTS

The Department of Justice is one of 15 **cabinet**-level departments that operate under the president. The DOJ handles federal law enforcement.

U.S. Attorney General Charles Bonaparte (left) and FBI Chief Examiner Stanley Finch (right) were the first leaders of the FBI. It was first called the Bureau of Investigation.

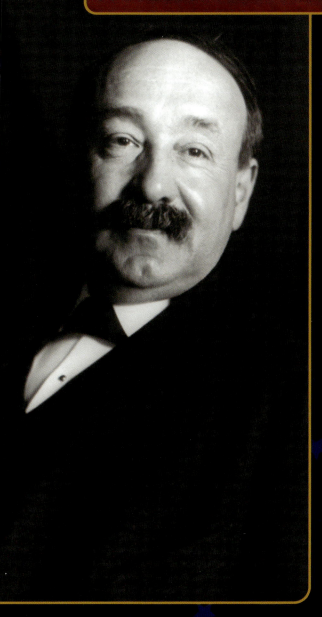

DEPARTMENT OF JUSTICE

The FBI is one of more than 40 organizations within the DOJ. The director of the FBI answers to the head of the DOJ, who is called the attorney general. The president of the United States appoints both the attorney general and director of the FBI. The U.S. Senate must then approve these appointments.

The DOJ is the top law enforcement agency in the United States. It's part of the executive branch of government. In addition to the FBI, many other organizations, such as the U.S. Marshals Service and the Federal Bureau of Prisons, work within the DOJ.

AGENCY INSIGHTS

There are three branches in the federal government. The executive branch is headed by the president; the legislative branch is made up of elected members of Congress; and the judicial branch involves the courts.

In 2025, President Donald Trump appointed Pam Bondi (left) as attorney general and Kash Patel (right) as the FBI director.

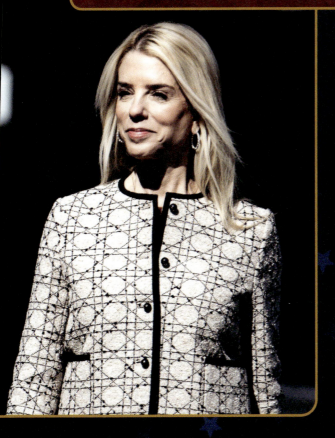

FBI BY THE NUMBERS

About 23,000 people work for the FBI, either as special agents or other professionals. Because there are so many employees and the country is so large, the FBI has many smaller offices and divisions. There are 56 field offices in major cities around the country. They each handle cases in the areas near them. There are also hundreds of smaller offices called resident agencies and even 23 offices in other countries.

On top of that, there are several divisions in the FBI that handle specific kinds of cases. For example, the **Counterterrorism** Division investigates extremist threats to the United States. The Cyber Division protects against attacks on the nation's computers.

AGENCY INSIGHTS
The FBI's total funding is about $2.2 billion each year!

Cyber criminals may target individuals, large companies and organizations, and even government bodies.

13

BAPTIST STREET CHURCH BOMBING

The FBI has investigated many famous cases since it was founded more than a century ago. One of the most well-known is the Baptist Street Church bombing. On September 15, 1963, a bomb exploded in the church, killing four young Black girls and injuring 20 others.

It was a clear act of hate against the Black community in Birmingham, Alabama. Because **civil rights** are protected by federal law, the FBI took on the case. Dozens of FBI agents interviewed thousands of people. It took decades, but the three people behind the bombings, all members of the Ku Klux Klan, were eventually put in prison for the crime.

AGENCY INSIGHTS

The Ku Klux Klan is a racist hate group. For decades, the FBI has worked to **disrupt** the group and prevent crimes committed by members.

A memorial to the four girls killed in the Baptist Street Church bombing stands in a park near the church. The girls' names were Addie Mae Collins, Carol Denise McNair, Carole Robertson, and Cynthia Wesley.

TECHNOLOGY

The Baptist Street Church bombing took a long time for the FBI to solve because the agency didn't have enough evidence. But in the 1990s, FBI agents found old tapes from listening devices agents had planted at one suspect's home shortly after the bombing. This led them to a conviction.

Technology and science play an important role in the FBI's investigations. They study DNA and fingerprints to help identify suspects. They use special cameras and computers to create 3D models of crime scenes. High-powered microscopes help them examine hairs, fibers, and other tiny bits of evidence they find.

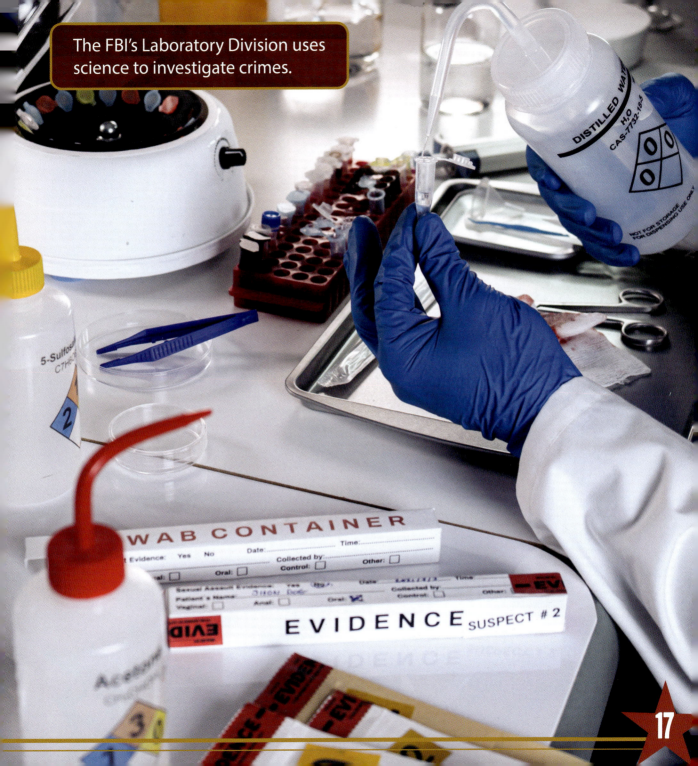
The FBI's Laboratory Division uses science to investigate crimes.

A CAREER WITH THE FBI

Because there are so many kinds of jobs in the FBI, you can take many different paths to a career within the agency. Becoming an agent requires a college degree, usually in criminal justice. Those interested in specialty jobs in the FBI, though, should research the right education path.

A degree in computer science or cybersecurity would be helpful for someone who wants to investigate technology-related crimes. Those who wish to work in a laboratory should think about an education in science. People with **psychology** degrees may be good at profiling or **negotiating** with suspects. Agents investigating **terrorism** cases would benefit from a political science degree.

In some cases, the FBI may help repay employees' student loans used for college.

If a job in the FBI sounds like it might interest you, you're in luck because the agency offers plenty of training. The FBI Academy trains new agents in Quantico, Virginia. Over 18 weeks, the agents receive 800 hours of **academic** study, **firearms** training, and real-life **scenarios**.

For young students still in elementary and middle school, the FBI has the Junior Special Agent Program. This course teaches young people about civics, crime prevention, and provides a glimpse of what life is like as an FBI agent. It's never too early to start learning about a possible career in the FBI!

AGENCY INSIGHTS

The FBI Academy is free, required training for all new FBI agents. Employees often return to Quantico for additional training later in their careers.

20

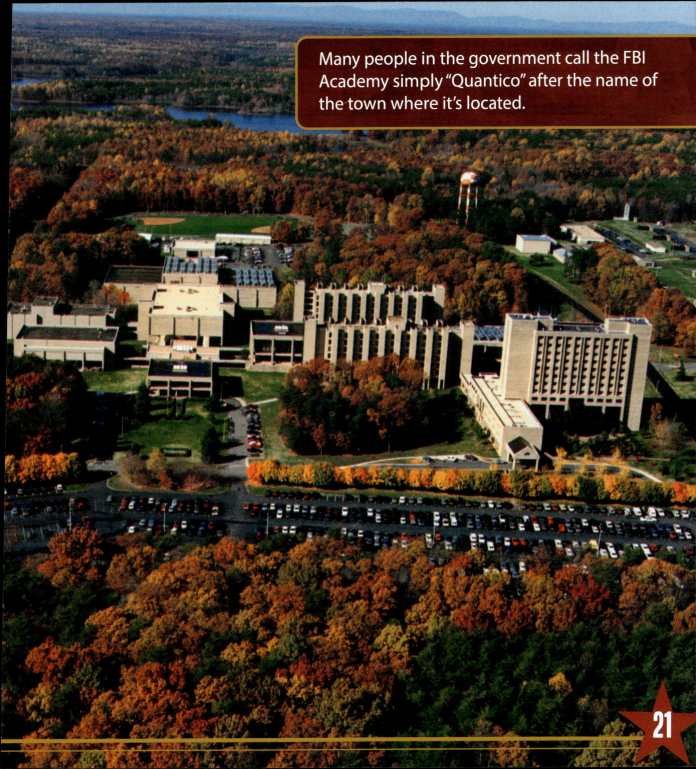

Many people in the government call the FBI Academy simply "Quantico" after the name of the town where it's located.

GLOSSARY

academic: Connected with a school, especially a college or university.

cabinet: A committee of government officials who help the president run the country.

civil rights: The rights of all citizens to equal protection and opportunities.

counterterrorism: Efforts by the government or military to stop terror attacks.

county: An area within a state that provides local government services.

disrupt: To break apart in a way that causes something to be unable to continue in its usual way.

firearm: A gun.

judiciary: Having to do with the justice system.

negotiate: To discuss something formally in order to reach an agreement.

psychology: The study of the human mind and behaviors.

scenario: A sequence of events.

terrorism: Using violence and fear to challenge an authority.

FOR MORE INFORMATION

BOOKS

Capitano, Madison. *FBI Agents.* Vero Beach, FL: Escape, 2021.

Gitlin, Marty. *FBI.* Mankato, MN: Black Rabbit Books, 2024.

Grann, David. *Killers of the Flower Moon: The Osage Murders and the Birth of the FBI (Young Readers' Edition).* New York, NY: Crown Books for Young Readers, 2021.

WEBSITES

Federal Bureau of Investigation
www.fbi.gov
Visit the official website of the FBI.

FBI: Baptist Street Church Bombing
www.fbi.gov/history/famous-cases/baptist-street-church-bombing
Read more about the FBI's case on the Baptist Street Church Bombing in Birmingham, Alabama.

Publisher's note to educators and parents: Our editors have carefully reviewed these websites to ensure that they are suitable for students. Many websites change frequently, however, and we cannot guarantee that a site's future contents will continue to meet our high standards of quality and educational value. Be advised that students should be closely supervised whenever they access the internet.

INDEX

A
attorney general, 8, 10, 11

B
Baptist Street Church bombing, 14, 15, 16
Bonaparte, Charles, 8, 9
Bondi, Pam, 11
branches of government, 10, 11

C
Congress, 6, 10, 11
Counterterrorism Division, 12
Cyber Division, 12

D
Department of Justice (DOJ), 8, 10
Director of the FBI, 8, 10, 11

F
FBI Academy, 20, 21
field offices, 12
Finch, Stanley, 8, 9

H
Hoover, J. Edgar, 5

J
Judiciary Act of 1789, 6
jurisdiction, 7

L
Laboratory Division, 17

N
name, 8, 9

P
Patel, Kash, 11
police, 4, 7

Q
Quantico, Virginia, 20, 21

U
U.S. Marshals Service, 6, 10